Historic England

Birmingham

Andrew Homer

AMBERLEY

First published 2019

Amberley Publishing
The Hill, Stroud, Gloucestershire, GL5 4EP
www.amberley-books.com

The right of Andrew Homer to be identified as
the Author of this work has been asserted in
accordance with the Copyright, Designs and Patents
Act 1988.

The publisher is grateful to staff at Historic England
who gave their time to review this book.

All contents remain the responsibility of the publisher.

ISBN 978 1 4456 9113 8 (print)
ISBN 978 1 4456 9114 5 (ebook)

British Library Cataloguing in Publication Data.
A catalogue record for this book is available from the
British Library.

Origination by Amberley Publishing.
Printed in Great Britain.

Contents

Introduction   5

Before the Industrial Revolution   6

Education and Learning   12

House and Home   20

Industrial and Commercial   29

Leisure, Entertainment and Sport   48

Public Buildings and Services   62

Religious Life   73

Transport Links   84

About the Archive   96

1728 — MATTHEW BOULTON — 1809
1736 — JAMES WATT — 1819
1754 — WILLIAM MURDOCH — 1839

Introduction

It is all too easy to think of Birmingham as a modern invention, a product mainly of the Industrial Revolution, but its origins go back much further. Traditionally, the name is associated with an Anglo-Saxon chief named Beorma who settled his people, the Beormingas, in a village or 'ham' around the seventh century, giving rise to the name Birmingham. By 1086 the Domesday Book valued the rural manor of Birmingham at just 20 shillings, but this was about to change. By 1166 Peter de Birmingham had obtained a royal charter from Henry II to establish a market between his castle, later a moated manor house, and the earlier St Martin's Church in the area now known as the Bull Ring. Peter's son, William, reaffirmed the market status in 1189 when Richard I came to the throne. By this time the town was officially known as Birmingham. The city of Birmingham grew up around this early market town and Birmingham Metropolitan Borough has expanded to encompass a wide area, including Sutton Coldfield to the north-east and the Lickey Hills to the south-west.

Birmingham is not known as the 'city of a thousand trades' for nothing. It flourished during the Industrial Revolution, inspired by such Lunar Society luminaries as Mathew Boulton, James Watt, William Murdoch and many others. For an area synonymous with manufacturing and industry it is surprisingly bereft of natural resources. For this reason, transport links such as the canal network and later the railways have always been vital for trade. Birmingham famously has 'more miles of canal than Venice'. It was a major centre for the Arts and Crafts movement, with both men and women working in the decorative arts and finding practical application in fields such as metalworking, stained glass, architecture and jewellery, as demonstrated in the world-renowned Jewellery Quarter.

The city of Birmingham, perhaps more than any other, has undergone almost continuous development. Some of this development was driven by social reforms to get rid of slum dwellings, some as a consequence of the extensive wartime bombing, but also a seemingly innate desire to sweep away much of the old and replace it with the new. As a consequence, many fine buildings, both old and not so old, have disappeared under numerous redevelopment schemes.

With just a few exceptions, the Historic England Archive provided all of the pictures used in this book. Therefore, the contents reflect what can be discovered about Birmingham within this extensive national archive. Consequently, it is a fascinating mix of the familiar and the not so familiar. For example, who would have thought that a Birmingham signal box is a building of national importance or that the architect of the Town Hall also invented a well-known form of transport.

Before the Industrial Revolution

Above: Sutton Park, 1926
Thousands of years of human habitation are evident in Sutton Park, such as the six Bronze Age burnt mounds excavated in 1926 near Streetly Lane. Part of a Roman road, Icknield (or Ryknild) Street, runs through the park connecting Wall (near Lichfield) to Metchley Roman Fort at Edgbaston. The Wyndley, Keepers and Bracebridge pools in the park were all originally medieval fishponds. (© Historic England Archive. Aerofilms Collection)

Opposite below: Metchley Roman Fort
Thought to be the only Roman fort in Birmingham, Metchley was situated between what is now the University of Birmingham and the Queen Elizabeth Hospital at the bottom left of the photograph. The earth and timber fort lay on a Roman road later to be known as Icknield (or Ryknild) Street. It was occupied by both soldiers and civilians at various times between AD 48 and around AD 200 when it was finally abandoned. (© Historic England Archive. Aerofilms Collection)

Kingstanding Barrow Mound

One of the oldest identifiable man-made structures in Birmingham, the barrow or burial mound at Kingstanding dates from the late Neolithic or early Bronze Age. This mound is 20 metres across and is said to have given the area its modern name. During the English Civil War, Charles I is reputed to have stood on the mound in order to review his troops.

Above: Weoley Castle

Although called a castle, this was really a medieval moated and fortified manor house, mostly dating to the thirteenth century. The castle was part of the Barony of Dudley and Roger de Somery was largely responsible for turning the earlier moated site into an imposing fortified manor house with its stone walls, defensive gatehouse, great hall and even its own chapel.

Below: Selly Manor

Originally known as Smythes Tenement, the house, pictured in its original location, was built as a farmhouse in the manor of Selly (Selly Oak) and is over 500 years old. After falling into a dilapidated state, George Cadbury purchased the property in 1907 and had it moved to Bournville. In 1917 the house, now called Selly Manor, opened to the public as the museum it is today. (Historic England Archive)

Above left: Primrose Hill Farm and Barn
At over 500 years old, Primrose Hill Farm and the barn at King's Norton are some of the oldest complete medieval buildings in Birmingham. The farmhouse was built in 1440 and the barn, pictured in 1977 before restoration, was built in 1457 according to dendrochronology (tree-ring dating) of the oak beams. (© Crown copyright. Historic England Archive)

Above right: New Shipton Farm Barn
Surviving records show that the original New Shipton Farm near Walmley in Sutton Coldfield dates back to at least 1433, but the present farmhouse is late eighteenth century. Pictured is the Grade II listed medieval cruck-framed barn, which is the oldest known in the Birmingham area. The barn is of A-frame construction with split oak trees forming the crooks. The felling date of the oak trees has been accurately established by dendrochronology to be 1424 (© Crown copyright. Historic England Archive)

Swanshurst Farm
The medieval timber-framed house on Swanshurst Farm survived right up until the early twentieth century, albeit by then in a very dilapidated state. Swanshurst had been the home of the Dolphin family for some 300 years until the death of bachelor John Dolphin in 1854. The farm building was demolished in 1917 and the associated barns in 1920 to make way for a new housing development. (Historic England Archive)

Above: The Green, King's Norton

A view across the green in the early 1900s looking towards the Bull's Head, the former Saracen's Head and St Nicholas's Church. In 1616 James I granted permission for King's Norton to hold markets and fairs. One of these was a 'mop fair' held on the first Monday in October where people could seek employment. The mop fair is still held on the green but is no longer a hiring fair. (Historic England Archive)

Above: Beginnings of Birmingham
This aerial photograph shows the area around St Martin's Church and the Bull Ring. It was a royal charter obtained by Peter de Birmingham in 1166 that first established a market 'at his castle of Birmingham' where the Bull Ring is now. The market lay between the original thirteenth-century St Martin's Church and the castle, which became Birmingham's moated manor house and survived into the early nineteenth century. (© Historic England Archive. Aerofilms Collection)

Opposite below: The Old Crown Inn
Pictured at the end of the nineteenth century, the Old Crown Inn at Deritend is the only surviving complete medieval building within the original manor of Birmingham. The late fifteenth-century building was the Guildhall and school for the religious Guild of St John the Baptist. It would have been a place for guild members to assemble as well as providing schooling and the services of a parish priest. (Historic England Archive)

Education and Learning

Old Grammar School, King's Norton

This two-storey building was originally built to house the parish library (given by Thomas Hall) and the grammar school, and was built by the parishioners for Thomas Hall (minister of the parish church) in 1662, reusing medieval timbers from another site (tree-ring dated to the mid-fifteenth century). In 2004 Birmingham's largest collection of medieval buildings – around St Nicholas' Place – won the BBC2 *Restoration* series, thus ensuring their preservation. This included the Old Grammar School, pictured here around 1910. In 1909 two female suffragists broke in to burn it down in protest, but didn't have the heart to do it! (Historic England Archive)

Right and below: Bishop Vesey's Grammar School, Sutton Coldfield
Founded in 1527 by John Harman (Bishop Vesey), the Bishop Vesey's Grammar School is another of the country's oldest schools. Originally situated close to Holy Trinity Church, the school, pictured from the air in 1928, was established on Lichfield Road in 1729. John Harman was born in Sutton Coldfield and became Bishop Vesey of Exeter. He was an adviser to Henry VIII, friend to Cardinal Wolsey and tutor to the future Queen Mary. Bishop Vesey's colourful tomb is in Holy Trinity Church. (© Historic England Archive. Aerofilms Collection; © Historic England Archive)

Opposite below: King Edward's School, New Street
Founded in 1552 by Edward VI, the neo-Gothic building pictured opened on New Street in 1838, replacing an earlier Georgian building. The architect was Charles Barry, who was assisted by Augustus Pugin. The pair would later work on rebuilding the Palace of Westminster in London. Demolished in 1936 as it was considered a fire risk due to being near to New Street station, King Edward's School relocated to Edgbaston, taking the hall with them. (Historic England Archive)

St Thomas's Church of England Day Schools, Granville Street
The Ladywood School was founded in 1831 with a two-storey building for the girls and boys departments and a single storey for the infants. By 1911 the accommodation was no longer adequate, and the 1917 extension pictured was built on Granville Street to house the mixed seniors. The school closed on 20 July 1967 and was subsequently demolished. (Historic England Archive)

Above left: Ikon Gallery, Oozells Square
The Ikon Gallery started life in 1877 as Oozells Street School. It was one of many such schools created following W. E. Forster's 1870 Education Act. The architects were the firm of Chamberlain & Martin. John Chamberlain would later go on to design the Birmingham School of Art. The building ceased to be a school in the 1960s and since 1998 has housed the Ikon Gallery. (© Historic England Archive)

Above right: Birmingham School of Art
Designed by J. H. Chamberlain in the Ruskinian Gothic style, it opened in 1885 as the country's first Municipal School of Art on Margaret Street. Under headmaster Edward R. Taylor, both male and female students focussed on practical art and design training heavily influenced by the Arts and Crafts movement and the ideas of John Ruskin and William Morris. The School of Art continues as part of Birmingham City University.

Above: Moseley School of Art

Designed by W. H. Bidlake in the Birmingham Arts and Crafts style, this was Birmingham's first branch school of art, opening in 1899. The school closed in 1976 but the building continued as an adult education centre for a few years before being sold in 1984. Past pupils include Roy Wood of Wizzard, Christine McVie of Fleetwood Mac and Peter Phillips, who co-founded the pop art movement. The Mosely School of Art has just undergone a major repair programme aided by a grant from Historic England. (© Historic England Archive)

Left: School of Jewellery, Vittoria Street

The decision to create a dedicated School of Jewellery was taken in 1889 at a historic meeting of the Birmingham Jewellers' and Silversmiths' Association. The school opened in 1890 in a former factory on Vittoria Street. By 1951 jewellery and silversmithing transferred from the Birmingham School of Art to create one dedicated school, which is now part of Birmingham City University. (© Historic England Archive)

Above: Wesleyan Theological Institution, Handsworth College
Pictured from above in 1920, the Wesleyan Methodist theological college was designed by architects Goddard and Ball in Perpendicular style. It opened in 1881 with forty students under theological tutor Frederick W. Macdonald. Extensions in 1931 included lecture rooms, a common room and a chapel. The college closed in 1970 but the buildings remain as Hamstead Campus student accommodation.
(© Historic England Archive. Aerofilms Collection)

Right: The Birmingham and Midland Institute
The Birmingham and Midland Institute (BMI) was founded in 1854 and had a key role in providing technical and scientific education together with literature and art for 'all classes of persons'. The original building in Paradise Street was demolished in the 1960s and the BMI moved to its present location in Margaret Street. This building, designed by architects F. B. Peacock of Cossins, Peacock & Bewley in the late 1800s, was originally the private Birmingham Library.

Above: University of Birmingham
Pictured from the air in 1928, the University of Birmingham was founded by royal charter in 1900 and was the first civic or 'red brick' university. It was the vision of its first chancellor, statesman and politician Joseph Chamberlain, to provide a university open to all. The original semicircle of buildings designed by Aston Webb include the magnificent Great Hall in the foreground and the iconic Joseph Chamberlain Memorial Clock Tower, known as 'Old Joe'. (© Crown copyright. Historic England Archive)

Opposite: Mason's University College
Viewed from Chamberlain Square in 1897 with the Central Free Library to the left, Mason Science College was founded by Josiah Mason and opened to students in 1880. The building was designed by Jethro Cossins. In 1898 it became Mason University College and in 1900 was incorporated into the newly founded University of Birmingham at Edgbaston. The Mason building was demolished in the 1960s to make way for major redevelopment work. (Historic England Archive)

House and Home

Perry Hall, Perry Barr
Perry Hall, pictured in 1913 when the South Staffordshire hounds had a meet on 18 November.
It was acquired by Sir Robert Stamford around 1569, who rebuilt an earlier hall. In 1669 it
became the home of the Gough and later Gough-Calthorpe family. After Perry Barr became part
of Birmingham in 1928, Perry Hall was subsequently demolished by Birmingham Corporation
to make way for Perry Playing Fields. (Historic England Archive)

Above: Aston Hall

The Jacobean mansion Aston Hall was built between 1616 and 1635 by Sir Thomas Holte. In 1643 Parliamentarian forces severely damaged the hall, including the great oak staircase. In 1817 the house was bought by bankers Whitehead and Greenway, who leased it to James Watt's son, James Watt Jr, who lived there until his death in 1848. The hall faced an uncertain future when Aston Park was developed in the 1850s. (Historic England Archive)

Right: Aston Hall

In 1857 Aston Hall and Park Company created a public park and museum, which was opened by Queen Victoria in 1858. By 1864 this venture had failed, and Aston Hall became the first stately home to come into municipal ownership when it was purchased by Birmingham Corporation. In 1897 Aston Villa moved onto part of the grounds, now Villa Park. The Grade I listed Aston Hall is now a popular visitor attraction. In the early 1900s it even featured the skeleton of a woman in a hidden room under the stairs! (Historic England Archive)

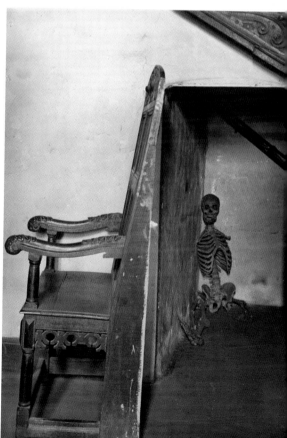

Above: Rookery House, Erdington

Built in 1727 for wealthy Birmingham banker Abraham Spooner, Rookery House has an interesting connection with the anti-slavery campaign: William Wilberforce met and married Abraham's granddaughter Barbara Ann in 1797. The house eventually became the Town Hall before Erdington became part of Birmingham in 1911. The Grade II listed house, pictured around 1920, was owned by Birmingham City Council, but was sold when it proved too expensive to maintain. (Historic England Archive)

Below: Soho House, Handsworth

The home of industrialist Mathew Boulton from 1766 to 1809, Soho House is now a museum. In partnership with James Watt, Mathew Boulton produced steam engines that helped power the Industrial Revolution. Soho House regularly played host to the Lunar Society, men of science and industry who met to discuss scientific and philosophical ideas. Members included James Watt, Erasmus Darwin, Joseph Priestley and others prominent in the Midlands during in this era.

Lench's Trust Almshouses, Ladywood

Lench's Trust dates back to 1525 when tanner William Lench willed his money to be used for charitable works. After 1838 the trust paid stipends (pensions) to the poor and also provided almshouses such as the group of twelve in Ladywood. Shown is the Grade II listed Matron's Lodge, built in 1858. A 1960s canopy protects the door. (© Crown copyright. Historic England Archive)

Above: Highbury Hall, Moseley
Built as a family home by Joseph Chamberlain, former Birmingham mayor and British statesman, Highbury Hall was designed in the Venetian Gothic style by the Birmingham architect John Chamberlain (no relation). It was completed in 1878 and remained the family home until Joseph Chamberlain's death in 1914. The house and grounds are administered by the Chamberlain Highbury Trust, who are committed to the preservation of the historically important house and grounds. (Historic England Archive)

Opposite above: Woodgate, Four Oaks, Sutton Coldfield
Woodgate, pictured in 1898, was designed and built by celebrated architect William Henry Bidlake for himself in 1896. He took great influence from the Arts and Crafts movement in the design of his houses but was also well known for his more Gothic-inspired churches. The 24 June 1911 issue of *Country Life* featured an illustrated two-page article devoted to Woodgate. (Historic England Archive)

Opposite below: Willow Street, Bournville
Bournville model village was the vision of chocolate maker and philanthropist George Cadbury and his wife Dame Elizabeth Cadbury. After purchasing land in 1893 a young William Alexander Harvey was appointed as resident architect to design the Arts and Crafts style buildings. Cadbury's idea of a 'factory in a garden' was realised and become an important influence on the wider garden city movement. (Historic England Archive)

Above: Ashcroft Estate, Nechells
New housing being constructed at Nechells in 1933. This was to be the Ashcroft Estate, which consisted of two-storey maisonettes. The land acquired by Birmingham City Council had been the site of the Duddeston Barracks, which survived until 1932. The barracks had been built mainly in response to the 1791 'Church and King Riots', better known as the 'Priestley Riots' after Dissenter Joseph Priestley. (© Historic England Archive. Aerofilms Collection)

Opposite above: Birmingham Back to Back Houses
Typical of industrialised areas, thousands of back to back houses with a shared courtyard, wash houses and outdoor toilets were built for working families in Birmingham. Virtually all are now demolished apart from Court 15, on the corner of Inge Street and Hurst Street. Preserved as a museum and administered by the National Trust, the Birmingham back to backs serve as a reminder of the harsh conditions working people lived and worked in.

Opposite below: Moor Pool Estate, Harbourne
Founded in 1907 by John Sutton Nettlefold, first chairman of Birmingham's housing committee, Moor Pool Estate was created on similar lines to Bournville, with low-density housing interspersed with green spaces. Pictured in 1956 are maisonettes on Ravenhurst Road. The architect chosen was Frederick Martin, who designed the estate with different types of buildings for variety but all adhering to the principles of the Arts and Crafts movement. (Historic England Archive)

Highgate Road, Sparkbrook
Birmingham was the third most bombed city after London and Liverpool during the Second World War. Both Birmingham and nearby Coventry were vital in supplying planes, vehicles and arms essential for the war effort. Sparkbrook, pictured in July 1942, was particularly hard hit due to its proximity to the Birmingham Small Arms Company (BSA) in Small Heath. (Historic England Archive)

Phoenix Prefabs, Wake Green Road
After the devastation of the Second World War there was an urgent need for temporary homes. The Emergency Factory Made Homes programme provided prefabricated houses (prefabs) that were only intended to last for ten years. The row of Grade II listed Phoenix-design prefabs in Wake Green Road made by John Laing, McAlpine and Henry Boot are believed to be the only surviving examples from 1945 still lived in. (© Crown copyright. Historic England Archive)

Industrial and Commercial

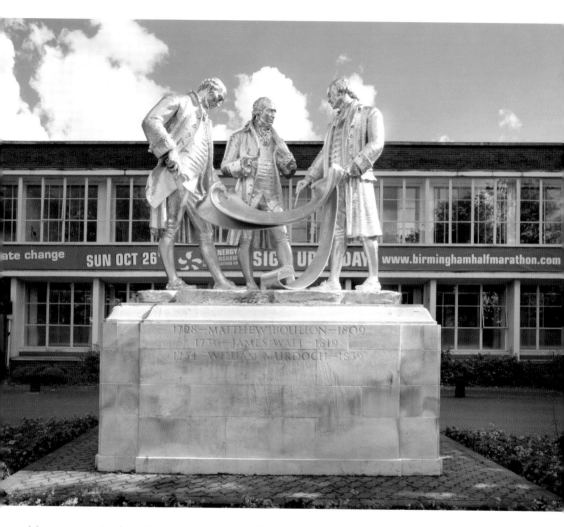

Monument to Boulton, Watt and Murdoch in Broad Street
Designed by William Bloye and Raymond Forbes-Kings, the statue was unveiled in 1956. Nicknamed 'The Golden Boys' or 'The Carpet Salesmen', it depicts Matthew Boulton, James Watt and William Murdoch. Matthew Boulton's manufacturing expertise, James Watt's improvements to the steam engine and William Murdoch's innovations in gas lighting made them world-renowned pioneers of the Industrial Revolution. (© Historic England Archive)

Above left: The Smethwick Engine
The Smethwick Engine is the oldest working steam engine in the world. Built by Boulton and Watt, the engine was installed in 1779 and used to pump water up a series of locks on the Birmingham Canal Old Main Line at Smethwick. This type of engine was the first in the world to employ both atmospheric pressure and the expansive force of steam. The Smethwick Engine is preserved at the Thinktank in Birmingham. (Courtesy of Birmingham Museums Trust)

Above right: Birmingham Gun Barrel Proof House, Banbury Street
An Act of Parliament established the Birmingham Proof House in 1813. It was at the request of Birmingham's flourishing gun trade that an official proofing house be established. In 1868 the Gun Barrel Proof Act made testing mandatory. This involved firing a 'proof' load of an overcharged charge through the gun barrel. The Grade II listed building was designed by John Horton and is both a working proof house and museum. (Historic England Archive)

Opposite above: Birmingham Small Arms Company, Small Heath
Founded in 1861, the Birmingham Small Arms Company (BSA) had opened their Small Heath factory for the production of arms by 1863. Pictured in 1917, both men and women can be seen working in machine shop No. 5 producing arms for the war effort. Rifles, Lewis guns, shells and military vehicles were produced during the First World War. During the Second World War BSA was bombed on 19 November 1940, causing significant loss of life. (Historic England Archive)

Opposite below: The Metal Workers' Arch, Colmore Row
When Queen Victoria visited Birmingham on 23 March 1887 a commemorative arch was erected across Colmore Row. The inscription reads, 'The Metal & Tube Trades Welcome Their Queen'. It was both Queen Victoria's jubilee year and the day before her birthday. She had been invited to Birmingham to lay the foundation stone for the Victoria Law Courts on Corporation Street. (Historic England Archive)

Above: Assay Office, Newhall Street
Birmingham Assay Office was founded in 1773 due mainly to the lobbying of Parliament by Matthew Boulton, who recognised the benefits to silversmithing and his own business interests. From its origins in three rooms above the King's Head on New Street, the office moved to Little Cannon Street in 1815 and then to Newhall Street (pictured) in 1877. The Assay Office moved again from its Grade II listed Victorian building to Moreton Street in 2015. (© Historic England Archive)

Left: W. H. Wilmot Ltd, Albion Street
The company was founded in 1860 by W. H. Wilmot in the Jewellery Quarter, moving to the Albion Street premises in 1893. Wilmot's specialised in watch bracelets, albert chains, necklets, bracelets and neckless chains in a variety of precious metals including gold. Pictured in 1897, the ladies in the workshop are surrounded by flags and bunting celebrating Queen Victoria's Diamond Jubilee. (Historic England Archive)

J. W. Evans & Sons, Albion Street

The silverware factory of J. W. Evans & Sons developed from a row of terraced houses and was in operation by 1881. The photograph was taken between 1902 and 1904 and it is interesting to note that men, women and children make up the workforce. The original historic factory has been preserved as a museum by English Heritage. (© Historic England Archive)

Gold Medal Diploma

In 1899 a gold medal was awarded to silverware manufacturer J. W. Evans at the Third Trades and Industries Exhibition in Birmingham. In the background of the Diploma representations of industry, mining, transport, energy, the arts and even air travel can be seen. Possible candidates for the figures include the Roman god Vulcan with his blacksmith's hammer and Diana, bringer of light, holding an electric light bulb. (© Historic England Archive)

Above: The Argent Centre, Frederick Street

Originally Wiley's Pen Works, the renamed Argent Centre was designed by J. G. Bland and completed in 1863. It was Birmingham's first flatted factory, designed for multiple occupation. In the nineteenth century Birmingham was the centre of the world's steel pen nib trade, having over a hundred manufacturers, such as W. E. Wiley & Co. The Argent Centre is now home to the unique Pen Museum. (© Historic England Archive)

Above: Argyle Works Building, Church Street, 1901
Printing and bookbinding company Buckler & Webb Ltd occupied the Argyle Works to the left. The very differently styled building to the right is St Phillip's Chambers. Pevsner's *Architectural Guide to Birmingham* describes this as looking like a 'fantastic castle in low relief'. Surprisingly, both buildings were designed by architects Newton and Cheatle and completed between 1898 and 1900. The Argyle Works has now been demolished. (Historic England Archive)

Opposite below: Newman Brothers Coffin Works, Fleet Street
In 1894, brass founders Newman Brothers moved to new premises in Fleet Street. By now they were specialising in high-quality coffin furniture, linings and shrouds. Newman's provided the highest quality coffin fittings for the funerals of Joseph Chamberlain and Winston Churchill, among many others. The company survived until 1999 and is now preserved as the Coffin Works Museum. (© Crown copyright. Historic England Archive)

The Custard Factory, Digbeth
Chemist Alfred Bird established his Birmingham chemist shop in 1837, later inventing the egg-free custard powder for his wife Elizabeth, who was allergic to eggs but loved custard! Egg-free instant custard proved so popular that by the end of the nineteenth century his son Alfred Frederick Bird was employing thousands of people on the 15-acre site. In 1964 production moved to Banbury and the Custard Factory is now a vibrant cultural centre. (© Historic England Archive)

Osler's Crystal Fountain, 1859
Designed by Follet Osler, the magnificent crystal fountain took pride of place in the reconstructed Crystal Palace at Sydenham Hill in London, which was opened by Queen Victoria in 1854. The fountain stood 27 feet high and contained 4 tons of glass. F. & C. Osler were crystal glassware manufacturers of Broad Street, Birmingham. (© Historic England Archive)

National Westminster Bank, Colmore Row
Designed by John Madin and completed in 1976, this was a bold statement of brutalist architecture. After it fell into disuse the building was eventually demolished, but not without efforts to save it. In the event only the unique aluminium banking hall doors, designed by Henry Haig in an abstract design based on the NatWest logo, were saved. (© Historic England Archive)

Longbridge Motor Works

Birmingham, and particularly Longbridge, was synonymous with the motor industry. Pictured from the air in 1929 is the Austin Motor Company. Herbert Austin acquired the site in 1905 and production commenced in 1906. During the two world wars, Austin switched production from cars to munitions and aeroplanes. The picture also shows part of the adjacent Northfield Aerodrome. (© Historic England Archive. Aerofilms Collection)

Fort Dunlop, Erdington

A familiar sight to motorists on the M6, Fort Dunlop was home to the Dunlop tyre factory. Developed during the First World War due to increased demand, the massive storage warehouse designed by Sydney Stott and W. W. Gibbings was completed in the 1920s. Fort Dunlop closed in the 1980s, but the locally listed building has been extensively redeveloped and preserved. (© Crown copyright. Historic England Archive)

The British Industries Fair Buildings, Castle Vale

For two weeks every year a former hangar at Castle Bromwich Aerodrome was the most visited attraction in the country. Established in 1920, the British Industries Fair was aimed at engineering companies and the central location and transport links ensured its popularity. The exhibition halls were demolished in 1960 to make way for the Castle Vale housing estate and were eventually replaced by the National Exhibition Centre. (© Historic England Archive. Aerofilms Collection)

Cadbury Brothers Ltd, Bournville

When the Birmingham Bridge Street factory became too small, George and Richard Cadbury purchased a greenfield site for a new factory and a new vision. They called it Bournville and it was to be a 'factory in a garden' with excellent working conditions, decent houses, recreation facilities and green spaces for the workers and their families. By the time this aerial photograph of the factory was taken in 1928, Bournville had become established as a garden suburb of Birmingham. (© Historic England Archive. Aerofilms Collection)

Left: Former Eagle Insurance Building, Colmore Row
One of the most notable Arts and Crafts-inspired buildings is the former Eagle Insurance building. Designed by Letharby and Ball, it was completed in 1900. Pevsner's *Architectural Guide* describes it as being 'one of the most important monuments to Arts and Crafts Free Style in the country'. Nowadays, it is possible to enjoy a coffee in this Grade I listed building.

Below: Council House Square, Birmingham
A view across Council House Square from 1886, although in 1901 it would be renamed Victoria Square. Opposite is John Corbett's Temperance Hotel, which opened in 1842. A self-made man, he worked his way out of acute poverty and fought tirelessly to end the many injustices inflicted on the poor. He was also an anti-slavery campaigner, but unlike contemporaries such as Joseph Sturges, his humble background more or less ensured there would be no lasting memorial after his death in 1868. (Historic England Archive)

Cobden Temperance Hotel and Coffee Palace, Corporation Street Architect William Doubleday designed the Cobden Temperance Hotel in the Gothic style for the Birmingham Coffee House Company, which opened in 1883. It was named after politician Richard Cobden, a confirmed supporter of the temperance movement and associate of Birmingham MP John Bright. The hotel was demolished to make way for a new Rackham's store, which opened in 1960. (Historic England Archive)

The Colonnade Hotel, New Street Pictured in 1883, the Colonnade Hotel is another of Birmingham's lost buildings. Designed by W. H. Ward and built in 1882, the building contained shops and offices as well as the hotel on the upper floors, which later housed Birmingham Chamber of Commerce until they moved out in 1961. The fine old Victorian building was subsequently demolished. (Historic England Archive)

Left and below: Grand Hotel, Colmore Row
The Grand Hotel was designed by Thomson Plevins for property developer Isaac Horton. Built between 1876 and 1878, by the end of the nineteenth century it had evolved into a luxury hotel. The paired Corinthian columns of the ornate entrance welcomed guests such as royalty, film stars and leading politicians to lavish events in magnificent rooms including the Grosvenor Suite (pictured). The hotel is currently under sympathetic redevelopment. (© Historic England Archive)

Above: Smithfield Market, Bull Ring
Looking across the old Smithfield Market in 1881. This had been the site of Birmingham Manor House. A steam-powered tram can be seen making its way towards Moat Lane and Upper Mill Lane with the Drover's Arms public house in the background. This area would later form part of the Bull Ring development in the 1960s. (Historic England Archive)

Right: F. W. Woolworth and the Bull Ring
Taken in 1962, this picture shows the original 1921 F. W. Woolworth threepenny and sixpenny store in Spiceal Street on the left, together with the new Woolworths superstore on the right. The new store was part of the Bull Ring development, which can be seen under construction. The 1960s Bull Ring was opened by the Duke of Edinburgh in May 1964. (© Historic England Archive. John Laing Collection)

Above left: The Rotunda, Bull Ring
Despite only being completed in 1965 and initially derided by many, the Rotunda, designed by James Roberts, has since become an iconic symbol of modern Birmingham. Originally designed to be only twelve storeys with a rooftop restaurant, a revised plan produced a twenty-five-storey cylindrical office block. Now Grade II listed, the Rotunda is no longer under the threat of destruction as it once was. (© Crown copyright. Historic England Archive)

Above right: The Selfridges Building, Bull Ring
Designed by architects Future Systems in 2003, the Selfridges store is a distinctive piece of iconic modern architecture. The dramatically curved structure is covered with 15,000 anodised aluminium discs on a deep blue background, which reacts to the sky and the surroundings. The style has been termed 'blob architecture' or 'blob-tecture' but, love it or hate it, the building has won a plethora of architectural awards. (© Historic England Archive)

Opposite above: New Street, City Centre
A busy day in 1895. Among the shoppers, two policemen can be seen patrolling and a horse-drawn cart loaded with barrels makes its way down the road. In the mid-1900s New Street had been the most fashionable shopping street in Birmingham. By the time this picture was taken the newly developed Corporation Street was rapidly taking on that particular mantle. (Historic England Archive)

Opposite below: Corporation Street
Corporation Street came about directly as a result of the 1875 Artisans' and Labourers' Dwellings Improvement Act and the vision of the mayor, Joseph Chamberlain. He used the act to clear away a large area of slums to create a Parisian-style boulevard to be called Corporation Street. Pictured in 1920, the busy street is crowded with shoppers and motor vehicles. (Historic England Archive)

Easy Row, 1900

Easy Row, pictured here at the junction with Paradise Street. Bellamy and Wakefield's pharmacy can be seen on the corner. The tall building is the Woodman, a much loved and lamented public house. It was known for its fine carving of a woodman, decorative tiles depicting Birmingham history and fine wood panelling. The Woodman together with the rest of Easy Row was demolished in the 1960s. (Historic England Archive)

Lewis's Department Store
Pictured from the air in 1950, Lewis's department store opened in 1885 as part of the new Corporation Street development. Planned in the 1920s, two buildings were linked by bridging across the Minories on Bull Street in order to create one huge store. Lewis's is still fondly remembered for visiting Father Christmas in the wonderful Santa's grotto. The store closed in 1991 when the company went into liquidation. (© Historic England Archive. Aerofilms Collection)

Leisure, Entertainment and Sport

UID'S WELL, SUTTON PARK. "SCOTT" SERIES Nº826.

Above: Druids Well, Sutton Park
The dog kennel-like structure photographed in the early 1900s was built to protect one of three natural spring wells in Sutton Park. Known as Druid's Well, it may have been regarded as a holy well, especially given that its alternative name is St Mary's Well. The spring ran down to Bracebridge Pool but is now very difficult to locate and the protective housing is no longer in place. (Historic England Archive)

Opposite above: Birmingham Botanical Gardens, Edgbaston
Designed by J. C. Loudon, the Botanical Gardens opened to Birmingham Botanical and Horticultural Society members in 1832. Local architect F. B. Osborne designed the bandstand in 1873, which can be seen to the left in the 1905 photograph. Osborne also designed the taller building in the background, Palm House, which was built in 1871. By 1884 the Terrace Range to the left had replaced the original glasshouses. Prominent politician Joseph Chamberlain was president of the society in 1876 and his son Neville was treasurer from 1902 to 1909.

Opposite below: Sutton Park, Sutton Coldfield
Now a Birmingham park, Sutton is the only one to have been a twelfth-century deer park. In 1528 a royal charter from Henry VIII enabled John Harman (Bishop Vesey) to enclose much of it for the benefit of the townspeople. Public enjoyment was stimulated by the coming of the railways in the later 1800s. Pictured around 1910, an Edwardian lady in a rather fine hat is sitting by the ancient Wyndley Pool, which had become a boating lake. (Historic England Archive)

Moseley Park and Pool.

Harborne, Queen's Park.

Stanford and

SOLDIERS MEMORIAL CANNON HILL PARK, BIRMINGHAM.

Above: Cannon Hill Park, Edgbaston, 1908
Louisa Ryland originally gifted the land for Cannon Hill Park to the people of Birmingham. Opened in 1873, it was designed by T. J. Gibson, who also designed London's Battersea Park. Pictured is a rare Boer War memorial designed in bronze by sculptor Albert Toft. Unveiled by Lieutenant-General Sir Ian Hamilton in 1906, it commemorates the 521 Birmingham soldiers who fell in that conflict. (Historic England Archive)

Opposite above: Moseley Park
Moseley Park and Pool belonged to the original Moseley Hall, which was burnt down during the Priestley Riots of 1791. If it had not been for the intervention of some local gentlemen who formed the Moseley Park and Pool Company Ltd, it would have been lost to development. The park opened in 1899 with access to key-holders on payment of a small annual subscription. A charitable trust continues the tradition to this day. (Historic England Archive)

Opposite below: Queen's Park, Harborne, 1905
Harborne Charity Fête Committee purchased the land for a public park through public subscription to commemorate Queen Victoria's Diamond Jubilee. The park was presented to Birmingham City Council when it was opened on 5 October 1898. To commemorate the coronation of Elizabeth II a sensory garden was created for students of the nearby Birmingham Royal Institution for the Blind, now called Queen Alexandra College. (Historic England Archive)

Golden Lion Inn, Cannon Hill Park, 1915
The Golden Lion Inn was probably built around 1575–1610 at Deritend, most likely as a clergy house. By the eighteenth century it had become the Golden Lion Inn. In 1911 the Birmingham Archaeological Society succeeded in having the timber-framed building moved to Cannon Hill Park for use as a cricket pavilion. The Friends of the Golden Lion are presently working towards restoring the building for future public use. (Historic England Archive)

Bilbery Hill Tea Rooms, Lickey Hills, 1907
Birmingham's Lickey Hills Country Park covers some 524 acres. The building pictured, which became the Bilbury Hill Tea Rooms, was gifted to Birmingham by Mr and Mrs Barrow Cadbury in 1904. The popular tea rooms were operating until the 1960s and the building is now used as a residential centre run by Birmingham Clubs for Young People. (Historic England Archive)

Picture Theatre,
New Street, 1911
Shoppers in Birmingham can
be forgiven for not realising
they have visited one of the
earliest silent cinemas in the city.
The Picture Theatre on New
Street was designed by Nicol and
Nicol in a very elaborate style.
Unfortunately, the auditorium
ultimately proved to be too
small and the cinema closed
in 1926. Architect J. R. Shaw
subsequently turned the cinema
into the Piccadilly Arcade.
(Historic England Archive)

Odeon Cinema, Kingstanding, 1935
The Grade II listed Kingstanding Odeon was built in 1935 and designed by the Harry Weedon office. The Odeon reflects the style of many cinemas of the day, with its symmetrical design and curved corners. Oscar Deutsch's great innovation was to build his Odeon cinemas in a recognisable house style, which was essentially art deco but also streamlined moderne. (Historic England Archive)

Above: Oscar Deutch at Kingstanding Cinema
Birmingham-born Oscar Deutsch (third from the left) next to his wife Lily at the opening of Kingstanding Odeon in 1935. Lily was interior designer for many of her husband's cinemas. Talking pictures were a very popular form of entertainment and the founder of Odeon Theatres Ltd had the intention of building an Odeon cinema on the High Street 'of every reasonably sized town in the British Isles'. (Historic England Archive)

Above: Queen's Head Yard, Steelhouse Lane
A photograph taken in 1875 when William Blandford was the landlord of the Queen's Head.
The entrance to the pub itself can be seen on the right. An interesting feature is the picture
of a Penny Black stamp above the door being used as the pub sign. The yard gives a good
impression of living conditions in the backstreets of Victorian Birmingham. (Historic England
Archive)

Opposite below: The Shakespeare Tavern, Theatre Royal, New Street, 1902
Since 1774 there have been four theatres on the site of the Theatre Royal. All but the last,
built in 1904, has been associated with the Shakespeare Tavern, also known as Bragg's Vaults.
Originally at the front of the theatre in the 1770s, for most of its life Bragg's Vaults was
underneath. The name came from two generations of the Bragg family who ran the cellar bar
until son George Bragg's death in 1900. (Historic England Archive)

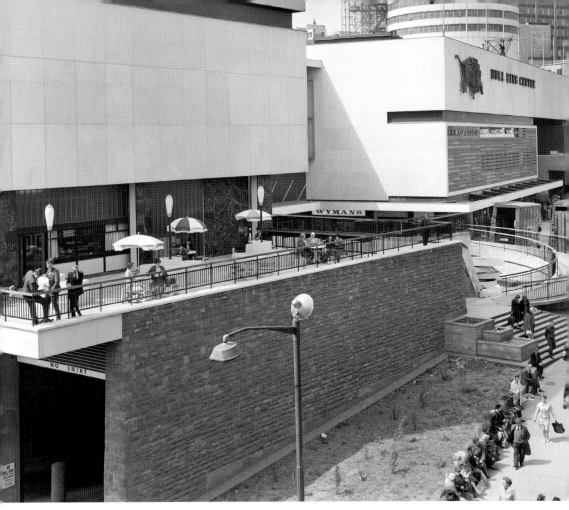

Above and left: Matador
Public House, Bull Ring
When the original Bull Ring
shopping centre was opened
by Prince Philip in 1964 it
included shops, restaurants,
banks and also public houses.
The Matador was one such
public house, and was built
in the same concrete brutalist
style as the rest of the Bull
Ring. Often described as
soulless and lacking in
atmosphere, nevertheless the
Matador, with its outdoor
patio and large function
room, is still remembered
with nostalgia by many.
(© Historic England Archive.
John Laing Collection)

Right: The Bartons Arms, High Street, Aston
One of the finest surviving examples of late
Victorian pub architecture, the Grade II*
listed Bartons Arms was designed by James
and Lister Lea for Mitchells and Butlers.
Original rooms such as the public bar are
decorated in superb Minton tiles featuring
both patterns and decorative scenes. With its
mahogany woodwork, stained and engraved
glasswork, snob screens and cast-iron
staircase, the Bartons Arms is deservedly on
CAMRA's National Inventory of Historic
Pub Interiors. (© Crown copyright. Historic
England Archive)

Below left and right: The Locarno Ballroom,
Hurst Street
The 1960s proved to be a thriving time for
Birmingham nightlife. One well remembered
venue was the Mecca Locarno Ballroom on
Hurst Street, which opened around 1961.
The 1960s version of the BBC's very popular
Strictly Come Dancing, then simply called
Come Dancing, had a show filmed there in
the lavish ballroom. Another claim to fame
is that the rock band U2 played the Locarno
in 1981, just when they were on the verge of
achieving international acclaim. (© Historic
England Archive. John Laing Collection)

Left: The Carillon, Bournville
A musical instrument in its own building.
It was a gift to Bournville by George
Cadbury in 1906. Originally consisting
of twenty-two cast bronze bells, it was
increased to forty-eight in 1934. The
instrument is played from a console
consisting of rounded levers called batons
and foot-operated pedals. It is played by
pressing the batons with clenched fists.

Below: The Rest House, Bournville
Designed by William Alexander Harvey,
the Rest House on the village green was
built to commemorate the silver wedding
anniversary of George and Elizabeth
Cadbury in April 1913. It was paid for by
employees of Cadburys worldwide as a
token of appreciation. The building was
intended to be a place of rest and shelter
in a busy world. It is now the Bournville
Carillon shop and visitor centre.

PART OF THE GIRLS' GROUNDS, BOURNVILLE—THE FACTORY IN A GARDEN

Girls' Recreation Grounds, Bournville, 1933

George Cadbury's vision was not just decent housing for his workforce but also that a tenth of the estate should be used as 'parks, recreation grounds and open space'. At a time when men and women had separate facilities, the Girls' Recreation Grounds and pictured garden with sunken pool was created in the grounds of the former Bournbrook Hall owned by George and Richard Cadbury. (Historic England Archive)

THE POOL, ROWHEATH RECREATION GROUND—BOURNVILLE

Rowheath Recreation Ground, Bournville

The thriving model yacht club at Rowheath Recreation Ground in the 1930s. This was an extensive leisure facility with sport's pitches, running track, bowling greens, lido, fishing lake and a large pavilion. Created by the Cadbury family, use of the sports facilities was free for their own workers and families. Due to Quaker George Cadbury's temperance ideals, Bournville has no public houses and only since the 1940s has Rowheath Pavilion Members' Bar been the sole place to purchase an alcoholic drink – members only of course! (Historic England Archive)

Above: Edgbaston Cricket Ground
Photographed from the air in 1938, Edgbaston was extensively developed in the post-war years to become the world-class cricket ground it is now. The Gough-Calthorpe family had developed Edgbaston into a smart suburb during the 1800s and the Warwickshire County Cricket ground fitted in very well with their vision. Calthorpe Estate land next to the River Rea was leased to Warwickshire and the newly created County Cricket ground's first match took place against the MCC in 1886. (© Historic England Archive. Aerofilms Collection)

Opposite above: Bournville Cricket Club, Men's Pavilion
In 1896 Cadburys laid out the Men's Recreation Grounds on the opposite side of Bournville Lane from the equivalent Girls' Grounds. Pictured is the magnificent Grade II listed Bournville Cricket Club Pavilion designed by H. Bedford Tyler and built in 1902 to commemorate the coronation of Edward VII. Both George and Richard Cadbury were enthusiastic sportsmen and often joined their workers in a game of cricket. (© Historic England Archive)

Opposite below: The National Indoor Arena
Built next to Brindley Place on the canalside, the National Indoor Arena (NIA) is pictured shortly after it was opened by athlete Linford Christie in 1991. The NIA was then the largest indoor space in the United Kingdom and a major venue for concerts, sports, conferences and exhibitions. Now known as Arena Birmingham, it was extensively renovated in 2014 and given a glass façade and three impressive sky needles. (© Historic England Archive. John Laing Collection)

Public Buildings and Services

Above: Victoria Square and Council House, 1901
The Council House was designed in a classical style by Yeoville Thomason and work started in 1874, the foundation stone being laid by the mayor, Joseph Chamberlain. The building was first used in 1878 but not officially opened until 1879. In 1901 Birmingham City Council decided to rename Council House Square as Victoria Square in honour of Queen Victoria. It was renamed on the 10 January but unfortunately Queen Victoria herself died just twelve days later on the 22 January 1901. (Historic England Archive)

Opposite below: Birmingham Council House and Colmore Row
A view from the 1890s looking towards Colmore Row. The Council House can be seen on the left and just visible on the right are the railings of Christ Church, which was demolished in 1899 and replaced by a row of offices and shop (Galloway's Corner), which were themselves demolished by 1970. At this time the square that would become Victoria Square was known as Council House Square. (Historic England Archive)

The Art Gallery and Council House from Chamberlain Square, 1890s The Council House was almost immediately extended after opening in 1879. The Tangye Brothers, wealthy Birmingham manufacturers, offered to purchase works of art to the value of £10,000, providing a new art gallery was constructed to house them. This was built on the Chamberlain Square side of the Council House above the new Municipal Gas Department offices. Yeoville Thomason was again the architect and the art gallery opened in 1885. The impressive Council House clock tower is known locally as 'Big Brum'. (Historic England Archive)

ART GALLERY, BIRMINGHAM, FROM MASON COLLEGE   9131   G.W.W.

COUNCIL HOUSE, & COLMORE ROW, BIRMINGHAM.

Above: General Post Office, Council House Square
Another view from the future Victoria Square in the late 1800s. The General Post Office in Birmingham is on the right of this late Victorian picture. Part of Christ Church can be seen on the left, which was demolished in 1899. The view is from the Town Hall looking down onto New Street. The post office was designed by Sir Henry Tanner of the Office of Works and opened in 1891. The building is now preserved as Victoria Square House. (Historic England Archive)

Opposite above and below: Birmingham Town Hall, Victoria Square
Begun in 1832 in the style of a Roman temple, the Town Hall was designed as a concert hall by Joseph Hansom (of Hansom Cab fame) and Edward Welch, primarily for the Triennial Music Festival. By 1851 it had been extended by Charles Edge, as in the 1913 photograph. Following closure in 1996, the interior, pictured in 2011, has been restored back to its original splendour. One famous story is that Lloyd George, giving a speech against the Boer War in 1901, was nearly lynched by a patriotic mob and escaped disguised as a policeman! (Historic England Archive; © Historic England Archive)

Above and left: Central Free Library, Ratcliffe Place

The first Central Library, designed by Martin and Chamberlain, opened in 1865 after Birmingham adopted the 1850 Public Libraries Act in 1860. This library burnt down in 1879 and was replaced by the building pictured. It was designed by J. H. Chamberlain in Lombardic Renaissance style with a magnificent high-ceilinged reading room. Despite efforts to save it the building was demolished in the 1970s in favour of a new Central Library. (Historic England Archive)

Above and below: Central Library, Chamberlain Square
The new Central Library, designed by John Madin, opened in 1974 as a striking example of brutalist architecture based on an 'inverted ziggurat' design. Madin's original plan was to face the building in Portland stone or Travertine marble to blend in with nearby civic buildings, rather than leave the concrete exposed. If this plan had not been abandoned by the council for economic reasons it might not have been demolished in 2016, only to be replaced by yet another new library. (© Historic England Archive)

Left and below: Victoria Law Courts, Corporation Street
The Victoria Law Courts were designed by London architects Aston Webb and Ingress Bell. The impressive building is faced in red terracotta, which was a popular material in Victorian Birmingham. Queen Victoria laid the foundation stone in 1887, her Golden Jubilee year, and the building was named after her. It was opened by the Prince and Princess of Wales in 1891. In contrast, the imposing criminal court, pictured in 1891, was panelled in dark oak with an oak canopy above the bench. (© Historic England Archive; Historic England Archive)

LL OF MEMORY, BIRMINGHAM.

Above and right: Hall of Memory, Broad Street

Opened by Prince Arthur of Connaught in 1925, the Hall of Memory was designed by S. N. Cooke and W. Norman Twist in Portland stone to commemorate Birmingham's dead and wounded in the First World War. It now includes the Second World War and all conflicts since 1945. Four bronze statues by Albert Toft represent the army, navy, airforce and women's services. Inside, a marble shrine holds a glass and bronze casket containing names of the fallen, and three carved plaques by William Bloye depict scenes from the First World War. (Historic England Archive)

Central Fire Station, Lancaster Circus

Pictured in 1937, the Central Fire Station is the triangular group of buildings around a drill yard left of centre. Designed by Hubert Humphries and Herbert Manzoni, it was opened in 1935 by the Duke of Kent. Doubling as the Fire Service Headquarters, it housed firefighters and their families with facilities such as a schoolroom and playground as well as garaging for the appliances. It ceased being an operational fire station in 2006 and has now been converted to student accommodation. (© Historic England Archive. Aerofilms Collection)

Birmingham General Hospital, Steelhouse Lane

In 1894, architect William Henman was appointed to design a new General Hospital in Steelhouse Lane to replace the Summer Lane hospital established in 1766. The picture shows the opening of this hospital in July 1897 by Princess Christian of Schleswig-Holstein, fifth child of Queen Victoria and formerly Princess Helena. She was a very active member of the royal family and became President of the Royal British Nurses' Association in 1887, making her the perfect choice to open the new General Hospital. (Historic England Archive)

Above: King's Norton Union Workhouse and Selly Oak Hospital
When this photograph was taken in the late 1800s the Selly Oak Hospital site was the workhouse of King's Norton Poor Law Union. Many hospitals had their origins in the 1834 Poor Law Amendment Act, which required the poor to be housed in workhouses. Basic needs would be met in return for hours of toil. In 1897 a dedicated infirmary was erected and by 1911 this had been renamed Selly Oak Hospital, which eventually closed in 2011. (Historic England Archive)

Below: Uffculme Hospital, Moseley
Uffculme House, designed by William Jenkins, was built for Richard Cadbury and his second wife, Emma, in 1891. The name comes from Uffculme in Devon. Richard died in 1899 and Emma in 1907 after a fall aboard the liner *Empress of India*. During the First World War Uffculme was used as an auxiliary hospital. In 1916 the house was gifted to the city council and used for psychiatric services until 1999. Following sympathetic refurbishment, the building is now a training, conference and function centre. (Historic England Archive)

Above: Winson Green Prison
Originally called the Birmingham Borough Gaol when it opened in 1849, it has long been known as Winson Green Prison. Designed by architect Daniel Rowlinson Hill in a Gothic style, anyone who remembers the old prison will recognise the castle-like structure of the main gate. Originally the prison had cells for 321 men, women and juveniles. Photographed in 1987, HMP Birmingham, as it is now known, has since been both enlarged and modernised to cater for 1,450 male prisoners. (© Crown copyright. Historic England Archive)

Left: The Pumphouse, Waterworks Road, Edgbaston
Built *c.* 1870, the steam-powered water pumping station was designed by J. H. Chamberlain and W. Martin for the Birmingham Waterworks Company. By 1876, the mayor of Birmingham, Joseph Chamberlain, was implementing his 'gas and water socialism' and the Waterworks Company was purchased by the council. J. R. R. Tolkien lived nearby as a child and the Pumphouse chimney together with nearby Perrott's Folly Tower are often cited as being the inspiration behind *The Two Towers* in *Lord of the Rings*. (© Crown copyright. Historic England Archive)

Religious Life

Right: St Peter and St Paul's Church, Aston, 1902

A church was founded here sometime before 1086. Together with the ancient church at Harborne, both have a claim to be the mother church of the whole Birmingham area. A church at Aston was included in the Domesday Book of 1086. At that time Aston was recorded as being valued at 100 shillings while Birmingham was only 20 shillings! The church as seen today was mainly rebuilt by J. A. Chatwin from 1879 onwards and is regarded as some of his finest work. (Historic England Archive)

Below: St Peter's Church, Harborne

Perhaps the stronger candidate for mother church of Birmingham, this was the site of an important Anglo-Saxon minster, as was Aston. The battlemented tower is believed to be at least partly fourteenth century, but nothing remains of the church prior to that date. The rest of the present Grade II listed building is Victorian, designed by architect Yeoville Thomason in 1867. David Cox, the great English landscape painter, is buried in the churchyard and also commemorated in the east window. (© Historic England Archive)

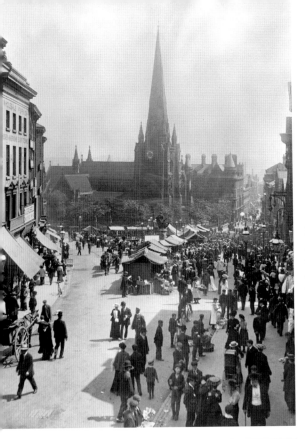

St Martin's Church, Bull Ring
A busy day in 1905. St Martin's Church overlooks the market as it has done for centuries. Its exact origins are unknown but there was probably a church in existence in the twelfth century, and certainly by the thirteenth. It is likely that this was the site of the first church in the ancient parish of Birmingham. Very little of this remains as St Martin's was completely rebuilt in the nineteenth century, largely by J. A. Chatwin, at which time it still had its churchyard, since lost to inner-city development. (Historic England Archive)

St Chad's Cathedral, St Chad's Queensway
Birmingham's second cathedral is the Roman Catholic St Chad's. It was built between 1839 and 1841 in the Gothic Revival style championed by A. W. N. Pugin. St Chad's became a cathedral in 1850 after Pope Pius IX reinstated the Catholic hierarchy in England and Wales. It had the distinction of being the first Catholic cathedral to be built in this country since the Reformation. In 1940 an incendiary dropped through the roof onto some central heating pipes. The pipes burst, extinguishing the incendiary and saving the cathedral from any further damage. A plaque bears the words 'Deo Gratias ['Thanks be to God'] 22 Nov 1940'. (© Historic England Archive)

Above and right: St Philip's Cathedral Church, Colmore Row

Originally the parish church of St Philip's, architect Thomas Archer constructed it in the English baroque style. Built between 1709 and 1725, it was consecrated in 1715. Yeovil Thomason redecorated the interior in 1871 and J. A. Chatwin extended the church in 1883–84. Chatwin was instrumental in obtaining the services of Pre-Raphaelite artist Edward Burne-Jones to design four magnificent stained-glass windows. In 1905 the new diocese of Birmingham was formed, and St Philip's became a cathedral, which is pictured here from the air in 1921. (© Historic England Archive. Aerofilms Collection; Historic England Archive)

Above left and right: The Bishop's House, Bath Street

A year after these photographs were taken in 1958 the Bishop's House was demolished. Designed by Augustus Pugin in what can be described as a 'domestic Gothic' style, it was built opposite St Chad's Cathedral in 1840 for the first Roman Catholic Bishop of Birmingham, Thomas Walsh. Pugin designed a unique spiral internal route from the front door to the adjacent Great Hall and screened passage pictured. This notable building was lost to the city's inner ring road scheme. (Historic England Archive)

Left: St Paul's Church, St Paul's Square

St Paul's Square in the Jewellery Quarter is the only remaining Georgian square in Birmingham. Centrepiece to the square is St Paul's Church, which is surrounded by houses fit for families of the industrial and commercial movers and shakers of the day. St Paul's was designed by Roger Eykyn of Wolverhampton and completed in 1779, although an addition to the tower and a spire was added in 1823 by Francis Goodwin. Money to build the church had been raised by selling the freeholds to pews. Both Matthew Boulton and James Watt owned their own pews in this church. (Historic England Archive)

Right: Holy Trinity Church, Bordesley
Holy Trinity was designed by Francis
Goodwin in the Gothic style and
consecrated in 1823. It is Birmingham's
oldest surviving example of a
Commisioners' Church, although it was
deconsecrated in the 1970s. It was paid for
by local subscription together with a grant
from parliamentary commissioners. The
Church Building Acts of 1818 and 1824
had made money available for the building
of mainly Gothic-style churches. (Historic
England Archive)

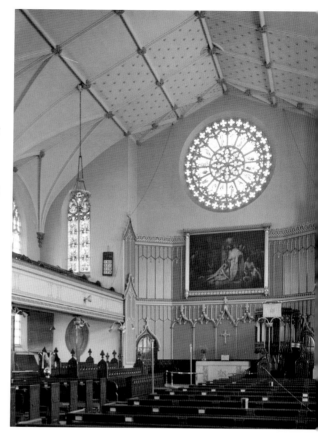

Below: Church of Our Lady Help of
Christians, Tile Cross
Built as a result of the Second Vatican
Council's edict on the design of new
churches in the 1960s, architect Richard
Gilbert Scott designed the Church of
Our Lady in a striking T-shape using
reinforced concrete. Completed in 1967,
the painter John Chrestian, who was a
friend of Richard Gilbert Scott, designed
the vibrant stained-glass windows that fill
the gaps left by the curved concrete roof
structure. (© Historic England Archive)

16. HANDSWORTH PARK AND CHURCH.

Above: St Mary's Church, Handsworth
Pictured behind the trees from Handsworth Park in the early 1900s is St Mary's Anglican Church, also known as Handsworth Old Church. An original stone church on this site can be traced back to the twelfth century. This later church has become known as the 'Westminster Abbey of the Industrial Revolution'. Buried and commemorated here are three giants of the Industrial Revolution: Matthew Boulton, James Watt and William Murdoch. All three are synonymous with the Soho Manufactory and the later Soho Foundry. (Historic England Archive)

Left: Holy Trinity Church, Sutton Coldfield
Holy Trinity has been modified and extended over the years, but the church can be traced back to the thirteenth century. The first recorded rector was Simon de Daventry in 1250. The church is closely associated with Bishop Vesey, adviser to Henry VIII, who founded the nearby grammar school. The tower, constructed in the fifteenth century, is the earliest part of the present church. Bishop Vesey extended it in the 1530s with north and south chapels, nave isles and its first organ. Bishop Vesey's tomb lies in the Vesey Chapel. (© Historic England Archive)

Right: The Birmingham General Cemetery, Hockley

Photographed around 1900, this was Birmingham's earliest non-denominational cemetery favoured by Nonconformists. Later called Key Hill Cemetery, it was designed by influential architect Charles Edge for the Birmingham General Cemetery Company and opened in 1836. The Jewellery Quarter cemetery has a number of notable graves including that of Joseph Chamberlain, politician and former mayor of Birmingham. (Historic England Archive)

Below: Warstone Lane Cemetery, Hockley

When Warstone Lane Cemetery opened in 1848 it was strictly Anglican, with buildings designed by James Hamilton and landscaped by Richard H. Vertegans. The cemetery features extensive tiered catacombs built in a sand pit. The catacombs were once open to the public, but due to noxious odours the Birmingham Cemeteries Act of 1846 required them to be sealed with lead or pitch. St Michael's, visible in the background around 1900, was demolished in 1958 but the Grade II listed Cemetery Lodge is now used as offices. (Historic England Archive)

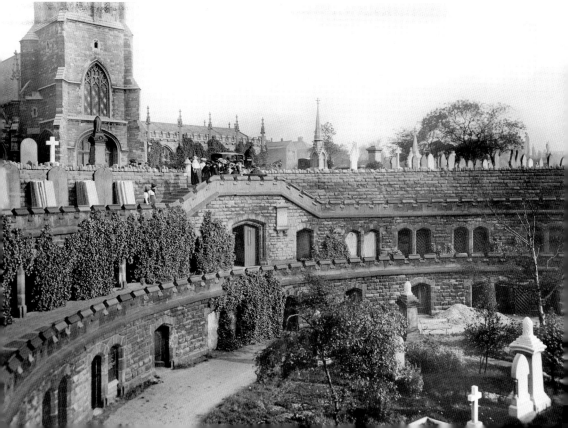

Left and below: Ramgarhia Sikh Temple (Gurdwara), Graham Street The former large nineteenth-century Highbury Hill Chapel in the Jewellery Quarter was built in 1844 and could seat 1,000 people. When the congregation moved to a new chapel at Soho Hill in 1879, popular preacher and later politician Charles Leach was invited to form an Independent or Congregational church. In 1913 the building was renamed Highbury Hall and in 1930 was purchased by the Elim Church. When they moved out in 1970, religious use of the building continued when it became the thriving Ramgarhia Sikh Temple. (Historic England Archive)

Right: Methodist Central Hall, Corporation Street
This 1904 Grade II listed building was designed
by Ewen and J. Alfred Harper in red brick and
terracotta, complementing the Victoria Law Courts
opposite. The main hall could seat 2,000 and there
were over thirty other rooms and three schoolrooms
together with a prominent tower. The Methodist
church vacated the Central Hall in 1990 and it
has suffered mixed fortunes since then. Used as
a nightclub for a while, the building is set to be
restored and reinvented as a plush hotel and leisure
complex. (© Historic England Archive)

Below: Birmingham Progressive Synagogue,
Sheepcote Street
Architect Ernest Joseph designed the Progressive
Synagogue in 1938. This building was a rare British
example of a synagogue designed in the international
style characterised by a lack of unnecessary
ornamentation, modern building materials such
as concrete and a flat, rectilinear appearance. As
this building was unlisted, it was unfortunately not
immune to city centre redevelopment and was finally
demolished in 2006. (© Historic England Archive)

Above and left: Singers Hill Synagogue, Blucher Street Designed by Yeoville Thomason in an Italianate style, the synagogue opened in 1856. It is known as the 'cathedral' synagogue of Birmingham and is the earliest surviving example of such in Britain. The synagogue was enlarged around 1937 by Harry Weedon and Partners, who also designed Odeon cinemas for the founder, Oscar Deutch. At this time Oscar Deutch was also president of the synagogue. In 2010 Singers Hill Synagogue won English Heritage's Most Improved Place of Worship in the West Midlands award. (© Historic England Archive)

Birmingham Central Mosque, Highgate

Birmingham Central Mosque was only the second purpose-built mosque in the United Kingdom. The project nearly came to grief through lack of funds but with the help of local communities, both Muslim and non-Muslim, by 1969 building and completion could take place, with the mosque formally opening in 1975. At that time, it was the largest mosque in Western Europe, accommodating up to 5,000 people on special days such as Eid. (© Historic England Archive)

Above left and right: The Friends Meeting House, Bournville
George Cadbury was a committed Quaker and had the Friends Meeting House built as part of his Bournville village development. The architect was William Alexander Harvey and the resulting building reflects the Arts and Crafts style rather than the simpler design ethic of many such Quaker meeting houses. It was built in 1905 and enlarged in the 1920s. A bronze bust of George Cadbury (by Francis Wood) appropriately enough looks out over the village green. The ashes of George Cadbury and his second wife, Dame Elizabeth, lie beneath the bust. (© Historic England Archive)

Transport Links

Above: Gas Street Canal Basin
The name Gas Street comes from it being the site of the gasworks, a substantial part of which still survives and is listed at Grade II* because it includes one of the earliest surviving gas retort houses in England, built in 1822. Gas Street Basin was the junction of the Birmingham Canal and the Worcester & Birmingham Canal. Operated by different companies, a physical barrier called the Worcester Bar separated the two canals until it was replaced by a lock and a toll system around 1815. With precious few mineral resources Birmingham was reliant on the canal network. Gas Street Basin would have been very busy with raw materials coming in and finished goods going out. (© Crown copyright. Historic England Archive)

Opposite above: The Roundhouse, Sheepcote Street
The Roundhouse is pictured to the left of the Birmingham Main Line Canal in Ladywood. It was originally used by Birmingham Corporation as stores and stables for horses. Appropriately enough the building, designed by local architect W. H. Ward in 1874, is built in a large horseshoe shape. After falling into disuse, the Roundhouse is now being preserved by the Canal and River Trust in conjunction with the National Trust. (© Crown copyright. Historic England Archive)

Opposite below: Warwick & Birmingham Canal Section of the Grand Union Canal
Originally, the Warwick & Birmingham Canal was a waterway in its own right, running from Digbeth to Warwick. It was officially opened in 1799 but began trading in 1800. In common with other canals it eventually faced fierce competition for trade from the railways. By the late 1840s the canal was in trouble, but it was saved in 1929 by becoming part of the Grand Union Canal, which stretches from London to Birmingham. (Historic England Archive)

Curzon Street Station, New Canal Street
The London & Birmingham Railway opened the first direct rail link between London and Birmingham in 1838. Curzon Street station, designed by Philip Hardwick in the Ionic style, was the Birmingham terminus, although passengers could swap platforms to the Grand Junction Railway to travel onwards to Liverpool and Manchester. The main building was designed to complement Hardwick's Doric arch at Euston. Curzon Street was superseded for passengers by New Street and after 1893 was used only for goods traffic until closure in 1966. (Historic England Archive)

The Queen's Hotel, Birmingham New Street Station
Pictured around 1901, a line of horse-drawn cabs can be seen waiting outside the station and the Queen's Hotel. Opened in 1854, the hotel, designed by William Livock in an Italianate style, made up one side of the station, which was opened on the same day and gave New Street a distinctive façade. The hotel was intended to accommodate increased passenger demand with originally sixty rooms over four storeys, although it was later extended. The hotel was demolished in the 1960s when New Street station was remodelled. (Historic England Archive)

New Street Station, *c.* 1900
The station itself was the work of the London & North Western Railway. A single-span iron-trussed arched roof covered the larger part of the station, and at 212 feet at its widest was the biggest in the UK when built. The station was shared by the Midland Railway and in 1885 a second section, separated by Queen's Drive, was opened to cater mainly for this traffic. In the 1960s it was demolished, and platforms covered by a concrete raft with buildings above them replaced what had once been such a grand station. (Historic England Archive)

New Street Station Signal Box, Navigation Street
While the 1960s concrete-covered subterranean station that was New Street garnered few admirers, the strikingly brutalist styled signal box is another matter. Built in 1964, it was designed by Bicknell and Hamilton in conjunction with the London Midland regional architect, R. L. Moorcroft. The five-storey building, squeezed into an almost impossible space, is clad in corrugated rough concrete with a projecting flat roof for shading. Grade II listed, the building is of national importance and described by Historic England as being very much a 'one off'. (© Historic England Archive)

Above and below: Snow Hill Station, Livery Street
Pictured in 1926 with trams passing by, the original 1852 station was a basic wood affair, and was not rebuilt in brick until 1871. Initially, the tracks supported both standard gauge and Brunel's broad gauge. The name changed a few times until the GWR chose Snow Hill in 1858. Between 1906 and 1912 a much grander station was built and incorporated into J. A. Chatwin's earlier Great Western Hotel. This was intended to cope with increased traffic and compete with New Street Station. Most of Snow Hill was demolished in the 1970s, only to be reopened in 1987. (Historic England Archive)

Above and below: Moor Street Station

In order to relieve the problem of traffic through Snow Hill Tunnel, Moor Street station was constructed to handle local trains and goods traffic. Opened in 1909 with temporary buildings, the station proper was not opened until 1914. The station was enlarged in 1930 and an extra platform built. Because of restricted space the station had two transversers installed that could move engines sideward, thus removing the need for reversing back to crossovers. Unlike the once far grander Snow Hill station at the other end of the tunnel, Moor Street has been refurbished in 1930s style. (Historic England Archive)

Above: Lawley Street Goods Station
Lawley Street originally opened as a passenger station in 1842 on the Birmingham & Derby Junction Railway. This was short-lived as the Midland Railway opened a new connection direct to Curzon Street in 1851. Lawley Street became a successful goods depot until a fire in 1937 and bombing during the war marked its decline. Pictured are delivery vans and drivers outside the Hartley's Jam Depot in 1927. (Historic England Archive)

Left: Hansom Cab in Stratford Road, Sparkbrook, *c.* 1900
The Hansom Safety Cab was patented in 1834 by Joseph Hansom, architect of Birmingham Town Hall. While in Birmingham he made friends with Dempster Hemming, who persuaded Hansom to patent his invention. It was both speedy and safe, having a low centre of gravity. The horse-drawn cab could hold two people with the driver at the back. Passengers spoke to the driver through a trapdoor in the roof. The cab was later modified and improved but always retained Hansom's name. (Historic England Archive)

Villa Road, Handsworth

Pictured in the early 1900s, four ladies are cycling along a very quiet Villa Road in Handsworth. By this time Birmingham was a major manufacturer of bicycles with companies such as BSA applying mass-production techniques. A vast improvement to the bicycle was made by John Boyd Dunlop when he invented the first pneumatic tyre. By 1902 Dunlop Pneumatic Tyre Company was producing tyres in Birmingham, later developing into Fort Dunlop. The row of shops the ladies are cycling past still exists, but the road is somewhat busier! (Historic England Archive)

Castle Bromwich Aerodrome

In a first for Birmingham, Alfred Maxwell successfully flew his monoplane in 1909 from what would become Castle Bromwich Aerodrome. During both world wars the airfield was requisitioned and in the Second World War aircraft, including Spitfires, built nearby were delivered to their operational squadrons from there. When this photograph was taken in 1936 the aerodrome served both civilian and military purposes. Castle Bromwich Aerodrome laid the foundations for both Birmingham Airport and the National Exhibition Centre with the move to Elmdon Airport in 1939 and the closure of the British Industries Fair in 1957. (© Historic England Archive. Aerofilms Collection)

Elmdon Airport Terminal and Control Tower, Bickenhill
By 1928 Birmingham City Council recognised the need for a municipal airport. Land was identified at Bickenhill and eventually Elmdon Airport was opened by the Duchess of Kent on 8 July 1939, accompanied by Prime Minister Neville Chamberlain. Pictured in 1939 is the combined terminal and control tower designed in art deco moderne style by Norman and Dawbarn. Built to represent aviation, 'wings' were featured on either side of the building. This would eventually become Birmingham Airport. The airport was Grade II listed in 2018. (Historic England Archive)

Birmingham Corporation Decorated Tram
Edward VII, Queen Alexandra and Princess Victoria visited Birmingham on 7 July 1909. Royal duties included opening the Aston Webb building at the University of Birmingham and also conferring royal patronage on the Birmingham Institute for the Blind. Everywhere they went was highly decorated to welcome the royal family, including the Birmingham Corporation illuminated tram pictured. The 'A R' either side of the crown probably refers to the queen, Alexandra Regina, in which case the opposite side of the tram would presumably be displaying 'E R', Edward Rex. (Courtesy of Birmingham Museums Trust)

DECORATED CAR,
RIRMINGHAM CORPORATION TRAMWAYS
ROYAL VISIT July 7th
Copyrigh

Birmingham Cable Tram
Opening in 1888, a cable tramway operated between Colmore Row and New Inns, Handsworth. Pictured is tram No. 175 making its way to New Inns. This was a non-motorised tram drawn along the track by a continuously moving cable operated by a stationery steam engine. The driver operated a clamp onto the cable to drive the tram and released it to apply the brakes for slowing down or stopping. By the early 1900s, the cable tram route had been electrified with overhead wires. (Courtesy of Birmingham Museums Trust)

Moseley Road Tram Depot
Taken from the air in 1921, Moseley Tram Depot was designed in 1906 for Birmingham Corporation Tramways as a showpiece service depot. The elaborate architecture of the depot is clearly shown from Trafalgar Road. A tram can be seen between the tram shed itself and the equally architectural offices on Moseley Road, which were completed by 1907 for an improved service. By 1949 the tram shed was being used by motor buses and it finally closed by 1975. Both buildings are now Grade II listed. (© Historic England Archive. Aerofilms Collection)

The Last Birmingham Corporation Tram
Birmingham Corporation tram No. 616 marked the end of an era. On 4 July 1953, the three remaining tram routes finished operations. Tram No. 616 on Erdington Route 2 was the very last tram. Rather crudely embellished with white paint, crowds lined the route and gathered at the Erdington terminus to witness the sad end of an era. However, trams were destined to return to Birmingham in 1999 with the opening of the Midland Metro. (Courtesy of Birmingham Museums Trust)

Above: The Five Ways

Even in 1921, when this picture was taken, Five Ways was a major road junction into Birmingham. The first mention of the name dates right back to 1565. The rectangular white building in the centre is Lloyds Bank, the original private bank having originated in Birmingham in 1765. This branch was designed by architect P. B. Chatwin and opened in 1909. To the left of Lloyds can just be made out the statue of Birmingham reformer and anti-slavery campaigner Joseph Sturges, which was sculpted in 1862 by John Thomas. This statue now stands in front of the nearby Marriott Hotel. (© Historic England Archive. Aerofilms Collection)

Opposite below: Salford Circus, Gravelly Hill Interchange

Gravelly Hill Interchange, or 'Spaghetti Junction' as it is more usually known, opened in 1972 and is Junction 6 of the M6 Motorway where it joins the A38(M) Aston Expressway. In an intriguing synthesis of old and new transport links, while traffic roars overhead the Walsall and Cross City railway lines pass beneath together with the Salford Junction of the Birmingham and Fazeley, Tame Valley and Grand Union canals. The pillars of the interchange had to be weaved around the towpaths to allow horse-drawn barges to pass through unhindered! (© Crown copyright. Historic England Archive)

About the Archive

Many of the images in this volume come from the Historic England Archive, which holds over 12 million photographs, drawings, plans and documents covering England's archaeology, architecture, social and local history.

The photographic collections include prints from the earliest days of photography to today's high-resolution digital images. Subjects range from Neolithic flint mines and medieval churches to art deco cinemas and 1980s shopping centres. The collection is a vivid record both of buildings that are still part of everyday life – places of work, leisure and worship – and those lost long ago, surviving only in fragile prints or glass-plate negatives.

Six million aerial photographs offer a unique and fascinating view of the transformation of England's towns, cities, coast and countryside from 1919 onwards. Highlights include the pioneering photography of Aerofilms, and the comprehensive survey of England captured by the RAF after the Second World War.

Plans, drawings and reports provide further context and reconstruction artworks bring archaeological sites and historic buildings to life.

The collections are housed in a purpose-built environmentally controlled store in Swindon, which provides the best conditions to preserve archive items for future generations to enjoy. You can search our catalogue online, see and buy copies of our images, as well as visiting our public search room by appointment.

Find out more about us at HistoricEngland.org.uk/Photos
email: archive@historicengland.org.uk
tel.: 01793 414600

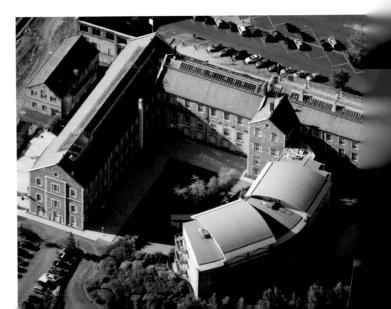

The Historic England offices and archive store in Swindon from the air, 2007.